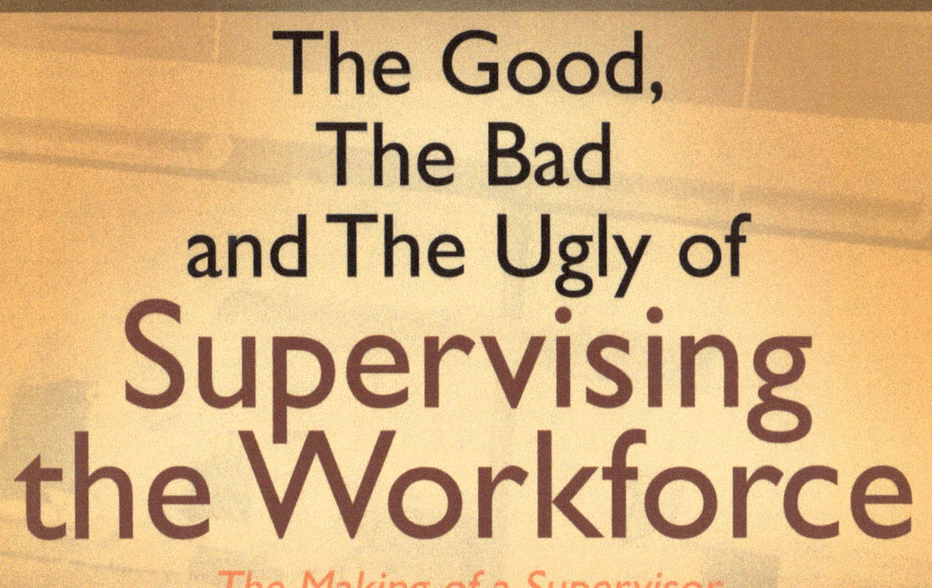

The Good, The Bad and The Ugly of Supervising the Workforce

The Making of a Supervisor

Bibi N. Bac

BIBI N. BAC, M.Ed., CFRA.

Ms. Bac, worked for the State of New York, Department of Mental Health, and holds a bachelor's degree in Business Administration and a master's degree in Adult Education. She is presently a Certified Florida Supreme Court, County, Family, and Circuit/Civil Mediator and Arbitrator.

As the former Director of Labor Relations and Associate Director of Human Resources, Ms. Bac advocate for NYS in the following areas:

....	**Discipline and Grievance proceedings**

....	**Human Rights and EEOC Complaints**

....	**Worker's Compensation, and**

....	**Unemployment Hearings**.

Ms. Bac work experience also includes but not limited to investigating workplace incidents, disciplining employees for conduct on the job and training thousands of NYS employees in various management training programs including the "Arts of Supervision."

One of Ms. Bac's many achievements includes the development of an Employee Handbook, detailing the facility's rules and regulations, policies, and procedures.

Ms. Bac is the author of "Transitioning from High School to the Workplace:" 2017., which is now available at Amazon, Barnes & Nobles, Books A Million and the Publisher, BookVenture Publishing Company.

For the past 13 plus years, Ms. Bac has been mediating court-ordered and private family and Circuit/Civil cases for the 20th Judicial District including mediating insurance cases for the Department of Financial Services.

TABLE OF CONTENTS

ACKNOWLEDGEMENT

No one has been more important to me in the pursuit of this project than the members of my family. Most importantly, my husband and my children.

THANK YOU

To all my co-workers, union representatives and my many teachers, instructors, mentors, and trainers who I have had the honor to meet and work with, I say "Thank You"; without all of you I would not have been able to develop and share my education, training, and experience in this Survival Guide for New Supervisors. My sincere thanks also go to Vicky Olson for editing the manuscript and Lynn Cadiz for her comments and encouragement.

DISCLOSURE

All the techniques and guidelines contained in this Book, is a combination of the author's education, training and experience including suggestions and tips gained from numerous seminars, workshops and courses taken from various academic institutions including from the following entities: NYS Department of Civil Service, NYS Governor's Office of Employees Relations and various joint labor-management training programs from Unions such as, AFL-CIO, CSEA – ASCME, Council 82 and NYS Management Confidential Training Programs.

DEDICATION

I hereby dedicate and give all rights to this Book to my husband, Andrew Bac, my children, Nadia Bac-Upeslacis & Nina Bac and to my precious grandchildren, Ashley and Avery Upeslacis, respectively. All Rights Reserved to them.

DISCLAIMER

This book is written about the author's 31 years of work-life experience in supervising, mentoring and training of the workforce. The Author does not offer any legal advice and should not be construed as such. In addition, the book does not contain all the information available on any of the subjects mentioned in it, and it was not created to be specific to any one organizational entity.

Every effort was made by the Author to be as accurate as possible, but there may be some typographical, omissions, inaccuracies or content errors. The author or the publisher does not provide any warranty or guarantee and is expressly excluded from liability for such errors, omissions, and inaccuracies. The use of any of the information contained in this book is entirely at your own risk for which the Author or the Publisher shall not be liable. This book is intended to be served as a Guide or a Reference for new Supervisors and for the purposes of education only.

Finally, please note that this book is written in "Simple Language" because my experience in managing the workforce has taught me that for staff to "get it" is to "keep it simple."

PREFACE

This book is a Survival Guide for New Supervisors. Readers will be able to explore some of the ins and outs of the trials and tribulations new supervisors go through as they try to manage the workforce and themselves. The knowledge, tips, insights, and suggestions outlined in this Handbook are priceless.

If you have no experience or training in supervising the workforce, you are in for a rude awakening. So, keep reading and see if you are ready to enter The Good, The Bad and The Ugly world of Supervision. Here are some of the topics referenced in this Book.

1. **TOPICS & SUBJECTS DISCUSSED**

Probationary Period for new employees

What management expects from supervisors

Supervisory Role, Responsibilities, and Expectations

Becoming a permanent employee

What to expect from staff, colleagues, and management.

Supervisory Accountability

Failure to meet Tasks and Standards

How to get promoted

Know when to quit before you get fired

What to do after termination

Supervisory Brain Teaser. What would you do?

2. **GUIDELINES FOR MANAGING THE WORKFORCE**

The making of a supervisor - First two weeks on the job.

Putting your right foot forward from day one.

Managing your work and yourself.

Selection & Recruitment, Delegating and Communicating with staff.

Making Unannounced Rounds and Time Management.

Monitoring Attendance, Performance Evaluation and preventing Accidents on the job.

Dealing with Insubordination, Anger Management,

Counseling -vs- Discipline and requesting Termination.

Avoiding conflicts and Sexual Harassment in the workplace.

Investigating incidents, interviewing staff, photographing the scene and collecting and bagging of evidence.

Writing investigative reports for management's review and action.

Samples of a Counseling memo, Recruitment & Selection form, Incident report and a sample of a statement.

BACKGROUND INFORMATION

For the record, this book has been in the making for several years. I wanted to include my experience, training, and knowledge to give my readers some idea of what it takes to be an effective supervisor. My intent is to put a personal touch to some of the workplace situations new supervisors will face as they transition into the workplace.

I know how it feels to be: passed-over for a promotion - dumped on - discriminated against, threatened, bullied and sexually harassed on the job.

As an employee and a supervisor for over 30 years, I have experienced many of the workplace situations mentioned in this Book including surviving the tactics used by some employees to sabbattach your work and stab you in back. I find these employees to be jealous, vicious, confrontational, threatening, insubordinate and incompetent individuals who would like nothing better than to see you fall on your face so that they can have the last laugh. DO not give them that opportunity.

Finally, if I can help one new supervisor to get a head start as they enter the world of supervision, I would have done my job.

A Word to Supervisors:

Some people say supervisors are born with certain qualities while others think these qualities are developed through work and experience. Based on my interactions with the workforce, I believe a good supervisor must have a little bit of both and a great deal of common sense. As a new supervisor, staff will be looking to you for guidance and help.

Having developed, implement and trained thousands of NYS employees in various management training programs including the "Arts of Supervision", I can tell you from experience that managing the different personalities in today's workplace, dealing with management issues and daily interactions with clients and customers, including irate, insubordinate and unprofessional employees can be stressful and at times downright frustrating.

Whether you work in a private corporation or in a governmental establishment, your behavior as a manager has a direct impact on staff performance and productivity.

If you are a new supervisor with no prior experience of supervising the workforce, this book is a must-have.

I wish I had a supervisory Handbook to guide me through when I first started my supervisory career. Believe me, it would have saved me lots of tears, stress, headache, embarrassment and unnecessary work. Hopefully, this book will help new supervisors to transition into their new role as a supervisor.

For starters, we will explore management's role versus yours and then review some supervisory procedures for managing your work and yourself, including what you can expect from the workforce.

SO HERE GOES

A: MANAGEMENT'S ROLES & RESPONSIBILITIES

As the CEO of a big corporation or the owner of a small company, you are responsible for instituting Policy and Procedures, Rules and Regulations for the workforce. To avoid chaos and conflicts in the workplace, management must:

Create a safe working environment for its employees.

Conduct orientation for all staff on the company's Rules and Regulations.

Give employees a copy of the company's Policy and Procedures Manual.

Train employees in the use of chemical products, running heavy equipment or the use of electrical products, etc. to avoid accidents on the job.

Investigate all complaints and grievances promptly and take corrective action, if necessary, even if it is only a rumor.

Give employees their due process before any action is taken against them for violations of the rules.

Have an open-door policy for employees to seek advice or help, and,

Have a ZERO tolerance for Sexual Harassment, Conflicts, and illegal substances in the workplace.

B: ORGANIZATIONAL CHART TO RESOLVE COMPLAINTS

Management must have a Chain of Command Chart in place for employees' complaints and grievances.

In keeping with the above, staff should be instructed to follow the CHAIN OF COMMAND to resolve workplace conflicts, for example:

1. All complaints and grievances should be in writing and given to the immediate supervisor for a resolution before going to the next step in the chain of command.

2. Employees should make every effort to speak to the person or to the supervisor to resolve the complaint before filing a grievance or going to the next step with the following exception.

3. **EXCEPTION:**

If the complaint is against the immediate supervisor, then the employee should go to the next step in the chain of command especially if the complaint is about "sexual harassment" against a supervisor.

4. **GRIEVANCE FORMS**:

In addition to the above, management must have a uniform system across the board in place for processing Grievances and Complaints, including a Standardized Grievance Form for employees to document their complaints.

Supervisors should be trained on the facility 's procedures for handling and resolving complaints including a time limit for a resolution and a written record of said resolution.

Note: Supervisors/Management should not retaliate against an employee for filing a complaint or a grievance against the establishment.

C: ORIENTATION TRAINING FOR ALL STAFF

Management must conduct orientation for new employees on its Policy and Procedures, Rules and Regulations. Listed below are some basic management's rules which should be included in any Orientation Program. For example:

RULE # 1   Call in and Sign in and out procedures, time off requests, meeting with employees' representatives and leaving worksite without authorization.

RULE # 2   Dress Code, ID Badge, use of safety equipment and unauthorized use of management's property.

RULE # 3   Incident reporting and cooperating in management's Investigations.

RULE # 4.   Soliciting, socializing, and sexually harassing behavior.

RULE # 5   Use of firearms, drugs, and alcohol on the job.

RULE #6   Work now and grieve later procedure and the consequences for refusal to carry out supervisory directives.

RULE # 7.   The requirement for updating addresses and phone numbers on file.

RULE # 8.   The requirement to submit to a mandatory health screening (IF appropriate).

D: MANAGEMENT'S EMPLOYMENT RULES

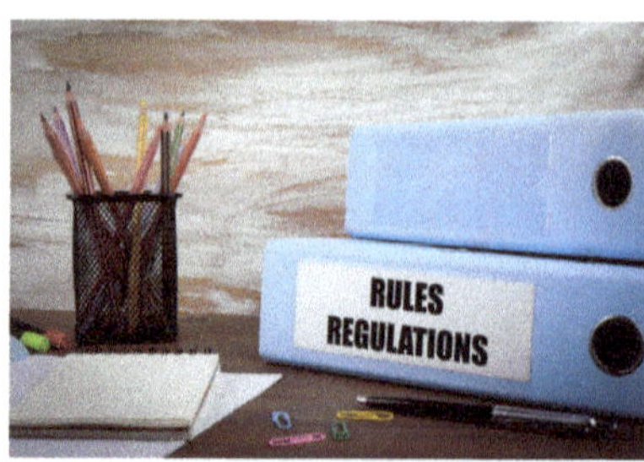

1. To avoid chaos in the workplace, management's rules must be designed to guide employees on how to behave on the job and what the standard of behavior is for the workplace.

2. Work Rules must be in writing and given to all employees upon appointment or during the orientation process. Management must secure the signature of all staff who were given a copy of the rules for the record. This will alleviate the problem of staff claiming that they were unaware of the rules when it comes to grievance and termination cases.

3. In my opinion, when there are **no written procedures**, supervisors tend to make up their own rules as they go along to the detriment of the staff as well as the company. This behavior has led in many cases for a very chaotic workplace, low morale, and production.

4. To correct this situation, management must ensure that its rules are:

    (a)   applied equally across the board, and,

    (b) employees are given their due process
        prior to any action taken against them.

5. If management fails to do the above, they can expect to be challenged at every step of the way including failure to prevail in grievances and in termination cases.

Chapter 2:   MANAGEMENT EXPECTATIONS OF SUPERVISORS

A: Everyone knows that some supervisors are good at somethings while others are not. It would be difficult to get someone with all the following skills. Nevertheless, management still expects and needs supervisors who can and are able to:

.... Connect with Their Staff

.... Have Great People Skills

.... Keep Their Cool Under Pressure

.... Have Good Listening Skills

.... Have Excellent Communication Skills

.... Know The Strengths And Weaknesses of themselves and their staff

.... Lead By Example, Don't Play Favorites,

.... Return Emails and Phone Calls Promptly

.... Don't Procrastinate, Be Accountable

.... Anticipate Problems Before They Occur

.... Never Assume – Check and Verify

.... Acknowledge Good Work

.... Give and Take Constructive Criticism

.... Defuse Conflicts Before They Become a Problem, Etc.

B: MANAGEMENT'S EXPECTATIONS OF EMPLOYEES

Whether you are a new supervisor or a new employee, management's rules have no distinction regardless of your **Rank**.

First: All employees are required to secure a copy of Management's Work Rules, and

Read it for understanding, do not assume.

Seek an explanation if you have questions

Follow all rules, do your job and grieve later if you must, and

Follow the Chain of Command Chart to file a complaint if you need to.

Second: After three weeks on the job, if you did not get your job description, ask your supervisor for one so that you can plan your schedule. This will avoid future problems regarding your attendance and performance.

Third*: ATTENDANCE & ASSIGNMENTS*

A: ATTENDANCE

Employees are expected to report to work appropriately dressed, alert and ready to start work. They should not start their workday by sitting at their desk drinking coffee or socializing in the company's break room while clients are waiting for service or help.

B: UNABLE TO REPORT TO WORK OR RUNNING LATE:

If you are **unable to report to work** as scheduled, you should call your supervisor at least one hour prior to the start of your shift unless it is beyond your control to do so. This will enable management to make alternative arrangements to cover your shift.

On the other hand, if you are running late, you should call your department to let them know how late you are going to be so that your supervisor can assign someone to stay for overtime to cover your area. (If you are a Time and Attendance abuser you may be required to produce documentation for future absences from the worksite.

C: BREAK TIME: Take your break/lunchtime when scheduled. If you need to change the time, get supervisory permission to do so.

SIGN IN AND OUT: Never let someone else sign in or out or clock in or out for you. Never sign-in or out nor clock in or out for anyone.

UNAUTHORIZED ABSENCE FROM THE WORKSITE: Always secure supervisory authorization before leaving your assigned area. **REMEMBER**, co-workers cannot give you the authorization to leave your worksite.

D: ASSIGNMENTS AND RESPONSIBILITIES:

NEVER REFUSE AN ORDER: Carry out all management's directives UNLESS you can show that it will put your life or others in danger. Refusal constitutes insubordination and may subject you to administrative action including termination from service.

COMPLETE ALL ASSIGNMENTS: If unable to complete your assignments you should let your supervisor/management know as soon as possible to avoid problems or consequences thereof.

E: VIOLATION OF MANAGEMENT'S RULES

Employees who violate any of the below-listed rules can expect to be disciplined up to and including termination from service. For example:

Engaging in a physical or verbal confrontation with co-workers, supervisors or visitors.

Using illegal drugs, alcohol or any kind of weapons or sexually harassing co-workers, supervisors, or visitors.

Fraternizing on the job especially with patients.

Spreading vicious rumors about co-workers, supervisors and management or posting workplace problems on social media.

Refusing to carry out administrative directives AND refusing to cooperate in management's investigations

Any misconduct off the job especially if you're a company driver or a representative of management, etc.

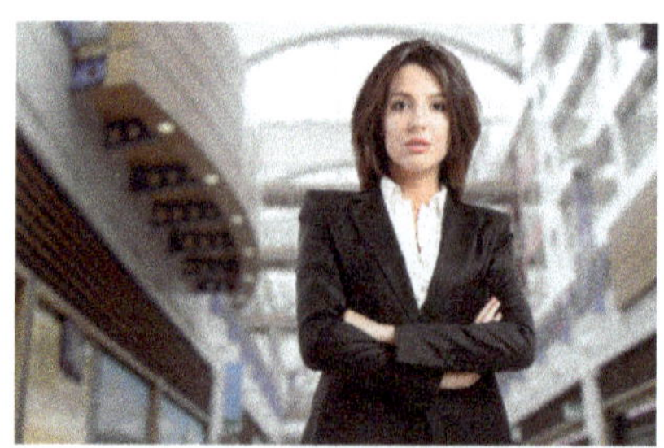

As a supervisor, you will have many roles and responsibilities. Listed below are some of the responsibilities which you may be called upon to perform depending on where you work. For example:

MAINTAINING MANAGEMENTS WORK RULES

MONITORING ATTENDANCE AND PERFORMANCE

DELEGATING & COMMUNICATING WITH STAFF

CONDUCTING STAFF MEETINGS AND MANAGING YOUR TIME

DEALING WITH DIFFICULT EMPLOYEES

PREVENTING CONFLICTS AND SEXUAL HARASSMENT

INTERVIEWING AND HIRING NEW STAFF

CONDUCTING ORIENTATION FOR NEW EMPLOYEES

INVESTIGATING INCIDENTS ON THE JOB

DOCUMENTING AND WRITING REPORTS FOR THE RECORD

COUNSELING AND TERMINATING EMPLOYEES, ETC.

PROBATIONARY PERIOD

B: Newly appointed supervisors can expect to go through what management calls a "probationary period." Most probationary periods can be 3, 6, or 12 months in duration. All through the probationary period, management will be checking your performance, your supervisory style and how well you are managing the workforce to see if you are a good fit for their establishment or not.

During your probationary period, management can at its discretion extend your probation, move you to another area, under a new supervisor or required you to attend a refresher course just to give you an opportunity to improve your performance.

In addition, if you are a productive and a responsible individual, who is honest, respectful, dependable, with leadership qualities, a team player, ambitious, and yes, loyal to the establishment, you stand a pretty good chance of being retained by management.

However, if you are a person who lacks initiatives, unable to control the work environment, gossiping with colleagues about management's directives or always watching the clock so that you can bolt through the door, sometimes even before the end of your shift, you can expect to be on the shortlist for layoff including hearing the two most famous words "You're Fired.."

BECOMING PERMANENT

If management is pleased with your supervisory skills, your performance, and your conduct on the job, you may become a permanent staff member of the company. However, becoming a permanent member of any establishment does not mean you cannot be demoted, transferred, disciplined, or terminated from your position.

If you are new to the company there are many office problems you may find frustrating. Supervising today's workforce is challenging, and painfully stressful. It takes a certain kind of individual who has the guts to take on the role of a supervisor. Let's see if you are one of these individuals

As a new supervisor, you may find yourself

.... Trying to fit in with your team and your environment

.... Having too much to do and not enough time to do it

.... Falling behind schedule because of a lack of resources or staff

.... Having problems with staff, colleagues and at times with management

.... Dealing with staff and assistants who are obstructionists, saboteurs, and backstabbers.

.... Dealing with conflicts and sexually harassing behavior, and

.... Dealing with insubordinate, irate, and unprofessional individuals, etc.

Chapter 4:   MANAGING THE WORKFORCE

A: To survive in today's ever-changing workplace, one must have the ability, training, and skills to manage themselves as well as others. As you are probably aware one of the MAJOR reasons' employees have a NEGATIVE attitude towards supervision is because of the actions of management. Few of us enjoy being confrontational with staff, but it is still a necessary part of the job.

My first encounter with a belligerent employee who was refusing to follow a direct order was terrifying. After speaking with my director about my experience with this 6'2", 250 lb., irate and insubordinate employee, he just looked at me and said, "Welcome to the job."

FLASHBACK FROM YOUR PAST

The shock of being promoted to supervisor finally hits you in the face. Suddenly you realized you have not been trained for this new position. Your mind started to wonder, "Do I have what it takes to make it as a supervisor?" "Should I just wing it as I go along and stand the chance of getting fired in the process?" "How do I go from being an employee to a supervisor?"

At his point, you are ready to pull your hair out. You wished that someone had invented a Procedural Guide or a Handbook for new supervisors so that you could get some help for what lies ahead. Well, don't panic, your wish has just come through. Hopefully, this guide will help alleviate some if not all your fears of surviving the workforce. Let's look at some supervisory styles and traits.

B: SUPERVISORY STYLES

Anyone who has had a supervisor knows that every supervisor is different. Some supervisors are layback while others are like the ones listed below, let's take a look.

FIRST - <u>Autocratic BOSSES</u>: Autocratic bosses are those supervisors who make unilateral decisions without gathering input from the work team.

SECOND - <u>Reactive BOSSES</u>: Reactive bosses are those supervisors with reactive personalities whose staff would be fearful to approach, even if they need help to solve their problems. Sometimes employees would make more errors by trying to come up with solutions on their own to avoid a difficult supervisor.

THIRD - <u>Controlling BOSSES</u>: Controlling bosses are those supervisors who only feel comfortable when they have total dominance over a group. These types of bosses intrude into areas not necessarily their level of control. Often, they will micromanage every piece of work and decision that comes out of the work.

AND then, there is the bad supervisor.

THE BAD SUPERVISOR

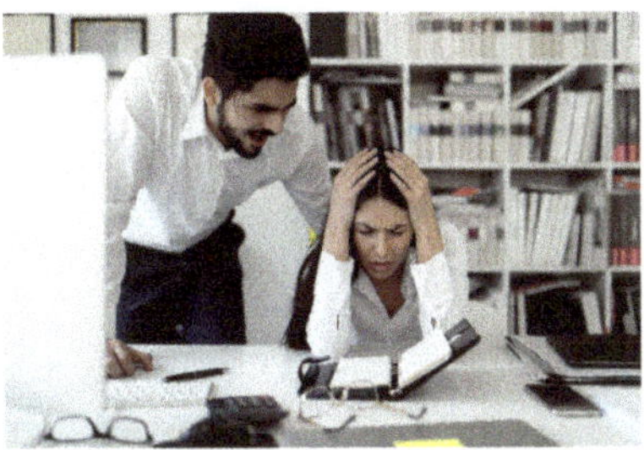

Have you ever had a bad supervisor who made your life so miserable that you didn't feel like going to work? Well, I have had a few. However, the knowledge I gained from these bad supervisors is priceless. Bad supervisory behavior makes employees feel demoralized, helpless, and at times, powerless.

Having gone through many supervisors in my 30 plus years working with NYS, I have found that bad supervisors treat employees unfairly for two reasons:

(1) Some supervisors do not know how to handle power, and

(2) Some supervisors feel threatened by their employees.

SUPERVISORY TRAITS

In my opinion, bad supervisors are usually, grumpy, resistant to suggestions, indecisive, unable to decide, moody, lazy, disorganized, inconsistent, incompetent, disloyal, lackadaisical, etc.

On the other hand, good supervisors tend to be more loyal, understanding, diligent, caring, competent, honest, fair, open-minded, pleasant, respectful, sincere, dependable, helpful, etc.

Many times, these "bad supervisors" do not last too long. They either get demoted or quit before they get fired. So, have some faith, he or she will soon be gone, and you will still be there.

Before we go any further, I would like to explore some of today's trials and tribulations situations happening right now in the workplace and see if you are ready to take the plunge or quit before you start.

If you are a present member of the workplace, I am sure you have experienced or are experiencing one or more of the following situations right now. Let's look at some of these situations.

First: WHAT TO EXPECT ON THE JOB

1. To be monitored by management.

2. Everyone will be watching you and most likely will be talking about you behind your back. Some may be good; some will be bad.

3. If you do not have your written job description, you will be doing everyone else's work.

4. You may feel like you are being "dump" on. Unfortunately, most new employees go through what I would call "an initiation phase" where at times it would appear like you are the only one working while others are enjoying a good laugh at your expense.

5. With regards to being "dumped on", I remember complaining to my boss about this very same issue. To my surprise, his response to me was "RANK has its Privileges." However, what I did not realize at the time was that by doing everyone else's job gave me the experience I needed to move up the career ladder when it came time for a promotion. So, don't get mad, take it in stride, you will have the last laugh. I did.

Second: WHAT YOU CAN EXPECT FROM STAFF

1. You can expect some staff will test your patience.
    Some will challenge your authority.
    Some will try to engage you in gossiping about others, just to see how gullible you are.
    While others will test your knowledge, hoping you would look like a fool in front of others.

2. **WHAT YOU CAN EXPECT FROM COLLEAGUES AND ASSISTANTS**

You can expect some display of jealousy from your assistant especially if he or she were passed over for your position.
Some of your colleagues may be gossiping about you.
Some will try to sabotage your work and stab you in the back the first chance they get.
Your assistant may run to management to complain about you, and play "stupid" when asked for an explanation.
They may even throw you under the bus and lied to save their butts.

3. **WHAT YOU CAN EXPECT FROM MANAGEMENT?**

Sometimes management takes it for granted that new supervisors have the knowledge and skills to manage the workforce and themselves. As a result, you can expect:
No orientation - No guidance - No buddy system
No one to show you around your new environment
No briefing on what's going on or what needs to be done
Work with your assistant or colleagues to get you to quit
Set you up for failure
Make you the scapegoat for their incompetence

4. **WHAT'S NOT TO EXPECT :**

If you are looking for a " pat on the back – "you're doing great"- "keep up the good work ",- "an outstanding Performance Rating" or a monetary reward - **you can forget it.** If you're lucky you might get an "effective" on your evaluation report even though you never missed a day of work and have given 110 %. each day while your ineffective, incompetent, do nothing, lazy co-workers reap your reward.

In my opinion, management's failure to recognize hard-working individuals can cause good employees to become disgruntled and ineffective to the detriment of the company's success. As someone who has experienced some of the above, my advice to you is to do your job to the best of your abilities and hopefully someday, somewhere, someone will recognize your hard work and reward you accordingly.

Third: Now let's look at a normal day on the job

 **H E L P**

A normal day on the job can find you with:

.... an employee whose negative attitude is affecting other staff

.... your 9 a.m. appt. is waiting in your office to talk to you

.... your secretary has decided to take a coffee break

.... your assistant is running late, as usual

.... your boss is on hold, waiting for you to pick up the phone, and

.... Clients/customers are waiting at the door to be served, etc.

 **NO PRIOR EXPERIENCE**

If you have no prior experience or training in managing the workforce, you will soon be knocking your head against the wall and sooner rather than later you will become like one of your disgruntled employees.

To help you transition from employee to supervisor I have listed some commonsense procedures designed to assist you as you go forward, starting with the **"Making of a Supervisor."**

A: PUTTING YOUR RIGHT FOOT FORWARD

One of the biggest problems new supervisors will face is the ability to overcome the obstacles that arise from the different personalities working together in one place.

Whether you were promoted from within or a new hire, you will need all the help you can muster to make your new job a success. As the new kid on the block, you will be watched by everyone. My suggestion to you is, for the first **TWO WEEKS** on the job, **DO NOT** do or try to change anything,

Instead, just:

.... Sit back, observe, and check out the office environment and the goings-on in the department. Ask questions if you must.

.... Acquaint yourself with the company's policies and procedures

.... Keep an eye on your staff to see who's working and who's not, and make notes of the ones you may want to have a chat with later.

After two weeks, you should:

1. Plan a date to meet with the staff to find out what the "Operating Norms" of the department are before you start changing things around.
2. Acknowledge what has already been done and ask the staff what they think needs changing or improving.
3. Communicate your expectations, work style and goals to the staff.
4. Do not just take over and force your ideas - good or not on the staff.
5. Clarify what your vision is and what the goals are for the department.

   Once it is clear, your staff would be adjusting quickly.

B: GET TO KNOW YOUR STAFF

Get to know some basic details of your employees, especially, their names, their skills, background, capabilities, etc. One of the problems I find with supervising the workforce is that many supervisors do not know their staff. Being aware of the skills or lack thereof of your team will enable you in the long run to match specific tasks with the right person.

Knowing your staff can go a long way in getting them to be more "Cooperative" and to work with you to get "The job done." Based on my own experience, I can tell you that there is nothing more challenging than you trying to achieve your goals through your employees.

C: RESPECT YOUR STAFF

You know the old saying "you have to give respect to get respect." Going around demanding respect because of your position will get you nowhere. Gaining respect from your staff is quite easy. All you have to do, is do what you say you would do, for example.

.... Listen to your staff and be honest in your response.

.... Stop snooping around the department or around your staff.

.... Let your staff do what they were hired to do.

.... Offer help, if it is needed, and give constructive criticism in private.

D: SET A GOOD EXAMPLE

Management rules are for EVERYONE including **supervisors**. Not only your staff must follow the rules, you too have the responsibility to do the same. Failure to do so will cause you NOT to be able to implement management's rules on your employees. If you break the rules, your staff will soon follow. What would you do then?

E: Lead by example.

- Follow the rules yourself. Do not play favoritism, this is one of the biggest pet peeves for employees. Train your staff on management's rules and regulations and explain your reason(s) for the exception to the rule. Discuss the Chain of Command Chart for filing complaints and grievances.
Give your employees a copy of the department 's policy. Have an open-door policy so that staff can come to you for help and guidance. Meet regularly with your staff to go over goals & achievements. Conduct on the job training, if applicable. Have a go-to-person so that staff can consult with, in your absence. Try not to be their "buddy", remember you're the boss.

F: SUPERVISORY RELATIONSHIP WITH CERTAIN STAFF

Caution: Becoming too friendly with certain staff can cause resentment among others and sooner rather than later your staff will lose all respect for you and nothing will get done.

Do not get me wrong, a good relationship with staff is very important, however, playing favoritism is another thing. If you do, you will experience what it really like to supervise a chaotic workplace.

If you cannot manage your workforce, you can expect management to come knocking at your door. Believe me, this is not a place you would want to be. So be careful with your interactions with your staff.

G: COMMUNICATING WITH STAFF

Communication between staff and supervisors is of the utmost importance when it comes to staff performance and morale. Therefore, when communicating with your employees, you should:

Be straightforward and direct in all communications, including written and spoken.

Listen when you are not speaking so that you understood correctly what is being said.

Keep your voice volume at a moderate level and avoid using an angry, threatening, or a demeaning tone of voice.

Give written instructions and clarify any misunderstandings to avoid future problems, Etc.

H: ALL STRESSED OUT

Workplace stress is unfortunately unavoidable these days in the workplace. We have all had at one time or another, heavy workload, too much to do with not enough time to complete the job, lack of support from management, no incentive or reward for a job well done, too many bosses, passed over for promotion, unfairness, lack of job security, etc., I can go on and on, but you get the picture.

SO how can supervisors help employees to relieve stress on the job? Simple: Supervisors can start by:

.... Thanking employees personally for doing a good job, either in writing, in person, or both.

.... Clarify any misunderstandings staff may have about their roles and responsibilities.

.... Allow employees to vent a little. It may ease some of their stress. Take time off to meet with and listen to your staff.

.... Create a working environment that is open, trusting and fun.

.... Create partnerships with employees by giving them a chance to grow and learn new skills.

.... Encourage employees to have a sense of ownership in their work.

.... Use performance as the basis for recognizing, rewarding and promoting employees.

Chapter 7:   ORGANIZING YOUR WORKPLACE

A: It is incumbent upon supervisors to have a fully functioning department regardless of whether they are in the office or elsewhere. No one wants to call your office and hear "She's not available." He's gone for the day", "She is on the phone, "Would you like to leave a message?" "Someone will call you back," etc. These are all frustrating answers, management, clients, and customers do not want to hear. To avoid these types of responses to callers, you should;

Train your staff on how to respond to inquiries, including resolving minor problems; where to look for information; who to go to for answers or guidance, etc.

Keep a daily, weekly or monthly tracking system to check upcoming events. Let your staff know where they can find important documents if need be.

Keep an updated list of all employees in your department or division, including telephone numbers, in case of emergencies.

Develop a system for departmental correspondence, filing system, including documenting telephone messages, incoming and outgoing departmental emails and the dissemination of information to appropriate individuals.

Keep a departmental binder of all employees' specific duties and responsibilities and train your staff to cover for each other in cases of absences or emergencies.

Delegate or appoint a team leader to supervise ongoing tasks or Projects.

Nominate a "GO TO" person for staff to go to for help, advice, or questions regarding upcoming issues or their work.

Keep your phone on when you are out of the department, just in case.

KEEPING THE WORKFORCE INFORMED

Conducting daily briefing with staff

B: Whether you work for a big corporation or in a governmental institution, you have a responsibility to keep your staff informed if you want them to represent you in your absence. I find a daily briefing with staff very useful. Believe me, it will save you lots of future problems with your staff and management. To do this you can plan to meet with your staff/or your Assistant daily to go over office Issues. For example, you can:

.... Limit the briefing time to 15-30 minutes.

.... Decide whether the daily briefing should be:

.... First thing in the morning, or

.... Last thing prior to the end of the shift

Before the briefing, you should have a list of upcoming issues to discuss with your second in command or your office manager.

Make sure your Assistant brings his/her Notebook for documenting the briefing for the record. Compare your notes with that of your Assistant to clarify any misunderstanding(s) prior to the end of the briefing.

At the next Briefing, you should review your notes with that of your Assistant from the day before to see what action(s) was taken or not and the reason(s) why.

The above information should give you an opportunity to make changes, reassign the task or act yourself to resolve the issue(s). This system will become your CYA just in case there is a question from management regarding your work or the supervision of your workforce.

LEAVE OF ABSENCE FROM WORK

C: You will at times have to be out of the office, due to illness, training or away on vacation. This should **NOT** mean that your office and your staff should be at a standstill until your return or not.

Listed below are some suggestions which you may find helpful in this instance:

1. Arrange a meeting with your staff to discuss your absence from the worksite.

2. Let your staff know your expected date of return to work.

3. Discuss the following with your staff/Assistant- a) What needs to be done in your absence-b) what to do in case of an emergency-c) what problem(s) may come up, and; d) how to administer the backup system in case of absences.

4. If your absence is NOT due to sick leave, leave a copy of your Itinerary in your office just in case, including any changes. Secure management's permission for your absence.

5. Give a copy of your itinerary to your superiors and let them know who will be in charge and where information can be found, if necessary.

6. (Optional) If appropriate, keep your phone on and touch base with your staff while you are away, just in case.

7. Let your staff know that they can call you in case of an emergency UNLESS you are out on extended sick leave or out of the country.

A: If you are **NOT an organized individual**, always **looking for stuff** on your desk, **can't find** what you need and **falling behind** on schedule, sooner rather than later, you will find yourself **running out of time.** Managing your time effectively can go a long way in relieving some of your problems including management off your back.

Listed below are some tips to help you to effectively manage your time.

1. Make a list and plan what needs to be done.

2. Prioritized all work and assignments either on a daily, weekly or monthly basis. For example, urgent, most important, and least important.

3. Decide what tasks or assignments can be delegated to subordinates or needs to be followed up by you later.

4. Check your list of tasks and make corrections as appropriate. Carry incomplete task(s) over to the next day or the next week if you are unable to complete any of the tasks outlined on your list.

5. To avoid distractions, check email and office mail first thing in the morning and the last thing before the end of your shift. This will enable you to not miss out on important office matters.

6. Return important calls and refer the least important ones for your staff to handle with written instructions.

7. Find some time during the day to be in contact with your assistant and or your secretary to see if there are issues which may need your attention.

8. Do not procrastinate

SUPERVISORY ACCOUNTABILITY

B: Supervisors are responsible for the welfare and safety of their employees while they are on the job. Supervisors are also ultimately responsible for the actions of their staff if it can be shown that they were negligent in their duties in managing their employees.

Listed below are a few pointers for new supervisors.

Never assume when it comes to your responsibilities. Remember the sayings, if you assume, you make an "Ass of you and me."

Make sure you get the facts and ask questions before you take any action.

Train your staff, check their work, keep your superiors informed, and document incidents for the record.

Keep an extra copy for yourself just in case. Remember proper record keeping is necessary and part of your responsibilities.

Do your research, be creative, consider- the "What IF." If not, you will soon find yourself on the "hot seat" with management and believe me that is NOT a place you want to be.

C: WRITTEN RESPONSE TO MANAGEMENT - STAFF- CUSTOMER

Never send a memo, email, or a letter out when you are angry or upset. Keep your cool and try to control your anger and frustration. I know sometimes it is very hard to do, I would suggest you count 1 – 20, take a deep breath and do the following:

Check and recheck your written document, talk to a friend, sleep on it and hope you may change your mind in the morning. Consider a one-on-one conversation with the person with whom you are having issues with to correct or clarify the situation. Once written correspondence is sent out you cannot take it back even if you try to recall it. Remember the person who receives it would have a hard time forgetting it.

In addition, DO NOT vent your disappointment or frustration about your co-workers, your staff, supervisors, or management on your Social Media, it may be used against you in the future. Pay attention to your surroundings and to whom you are venting your frustration. It will serve you best to keep your opinions to yourself or outside of the workplace.

D: ALWAYS REMEMBER TO... CYA...(COVER YOU'RE ASS)

When it comes to your job, it is important that you:

1) Consult; 2) Inform; 3) Report ; 4) Document; 5) Follow-up, and ,
6) Keep copies for the file. DO NOT forget to keep your own little "**Black Book**" to document important incidents with names, dates, times, place, subject matter, and a brief description of the events. It will be your "Ace in the Hole" to save your job.

Remember correspondence, office files or important records, etc., sometimes mysteriously go missing when it is most needed to prove one's guilt or innocence. **I can tell you from experience, people tend to have what I called "convenient amnesia". You will hear:**

.... **I don't know**

.... **You never told me**

.... **I don't remember**

.... **Where is it written**

.... **I wasn't there**

.... **I never got a copy, etc.?**

Unfortunately, if you are a supervisor, a manager, a teacher, a physician a CEO, or a Nurse Administrator, the BUCK stops with **>>YOU>>.** SO, always remember that little "Black Book" it will, in the end, save your **BUTT.**

E: LOOKING MOVE UP THE CAREER LADDER?

Here are some of my suggestions if you want to be recognized and get promoted.

Don't be a complainer. No one wants someone who is always whining, challenging and have a bad attitude when spoken to by supervisor/ management or someone who has conflicts with his or her employees or colleagues.

Be a team player. Go along and get along with everyone especially management.

Learn as much as you, including that of others and your bosses job.

Do not vent your frustration to your colleagues or your staff or on your social media, even if you felt that you have been mistreated.

Show restraint. Watch your body language when dealing with staff and management.

Offer to help your colleagues and management, do not wait for them to ask for your help.

Come to work early and **stay late** if you must to reach deadlines and complete all assigned tasks.

Demonstrate that you can manage the company in case of an emergency or the shortage of staff.

Give a hundred and ten percent **(110%)** to the job.

Welcome changes in the department including training and mentoring inexperienced staff.

Be a role model for your employees and other supervisors.

Consider taking additional courses online and attend seminars and workshops to develop other skills and knowledge just in case there is an upcoming promotional vacancy and **update** your resume accordingly.

THE FOLLOWING CHAPTERS ARE SOME WORKPLACE PROCEDURES FOR NEW SUPERVISOR

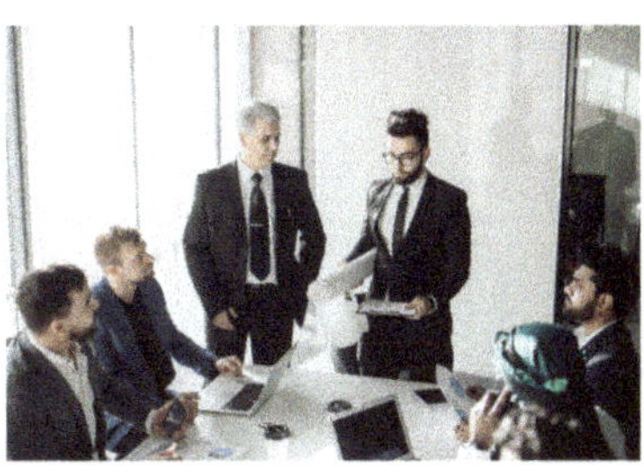

A: DELEGATING RESPONSIBILITIES

Despite the many advantages of delegating, some managers refuse to delegate because of:

Lack of time – no time to train

Perfectionism– fear of mistakes or lack confidence in their staff

Fear of surrendering some of their authority

Lack of trust in their staff to do the job

Whether you like it or not, sometimes, you will have to give up some of your power to your subordinates. Delegating is part of the job and necessary to keep the workflow moving: However, delegating too much of your responsibilities to staff may cause resentment in the workplace and problems for you.

B: IF YOU MUST DELEGATE, DO THE FOLLOWING:

Define the task to be done. Select the individual or the team you feel would be best suited for the task. Put a due date and time on the request. Log the task on an assignment sheet and anticipate what resources are needed.

Explain the reason(s) for the assignment to the staff /team. Discuss the required goal(s), results, and expected outcome(s). Agree on deadlines and confirm understanding.

Follow-up and support the project and communicate progress to your superior.

Let the staff know the consequences of failure to complete the task.

If more time is needed, try to facilitate, and negotiate a new deadline date and document the change for the record.

B: STAFF MEETINGS

Supervisors have a responsibility to meet and share information, discuss problems and future goals and achievements of the company with their staff.

There are several ways to share information with staff, for example

If time is of the essence, you can always communicate with your staff via an email or a memo. You can also communicate the information to your Assistant and have he or she delivers the information to the staff.

On the other hand, if a meeting is necessary, you should plan the agenda, decide the topics and goals to be reviewed, including who will address which topic(s).

Set a convenient date, time, and place for the meeting and assign a recorder to take the minutes of the meeting.

Send the Agenda to the staff before the meeting.

At the meeting, you should agree on a date and time for further discussions on all unresolved issues.

Send copies of the minutes to all who attended the meeting including your supervisor and, file a copy of the minutes for the record.

C: COMMUNICATING CHANGES IN THE WORKPLACE

The number one problem at work between management and staff is usually "poor communication." Lack of communication, feedback and follow-up are SOME of the biggest problems facing businesses today.

Experience has taught me that employees work better when they are informed and/or consulted about changes in the workplace, ESPECIALLY if the change will affect their jobs.

Management has the right to do what they believe is good for their stockholders and their companies, nevertheless, ignoring employees right to know if it affects their job is another thing.

D: To avoid problems, supervisors should:

.... Meet with and explain management's new directives to the workforce.

.... Give the staff some specifics and be prepared to explain why management feels it is necessary to implement such initiatives.

.... Listen carefully to the employees and try not to interrupt. Try speaking to the staff rather than speaking at them.

.... Watch your body language, your tone, and facial expression you do not want to send the wrong message to the staff.

.... Thank the staff for their input and let them know that you will bring their concerns to management's attention.

Once you are notified that you will be getting a new staff member, it then becomes your responsibility to;

A: Plan ahead to receive the new employee:

Open a personnel file for the new employee. Have a copy of the employee's appointment letter and references

Have a workstation ready and let your staff know that a new employee will be joining the team.

Plan for the new employee to shadow a senior staff of the department for at least two weeks, and, designate a go-to person for advice or help

B: WELCOME THE NEW EMPLOYEE TO THE DEPARTMENT

Introduce the new employee to the staff/team.

Explain to the employee that he or she will be shadowing a senior member of the team for at least two weeks. Let the employee know that you will meet again to go over assignments and work location after that. Give the employee a copy of the department's Policy and Procedures. Let the employee know who to "go-to" for clarification or questions concerning department issues.

C: Discuss the following with the employee.

Work hours, timesheets and sign-in and out policy, lunch breaks, requesting leave, dress code, departmental regulations, safety and emergency procedures, telephone usage, office mail, secretarial help, questions for HR, completing assignments, obtaining office supplies, work orders, equipment, etc.

Assign someone to take the new employee on a tour of the facility including the location for office supplies, restroom, cafeteria, and parking.

D: AFTER TWO WEEKS

Meet again with the employee AND give the employee his or her written tasks, standards and expectations.

Explain the probationary period and the performance evaluation process. Assign the employee to a work location and a supervisor.

DISCUSS THE WORK NOW AND GRIEVE LATER RULE

Remind the employee that all management orders must be carried out UNLESS such order will put the employee or others' lives in danger.

Let the employee know that failure to carry out management's orders or directives is considered an act of insubordination which may lead to disciplinary action.

Set a date and time for the three months review and let the employee know that you are available to answer questions which may arise on the job. Make sure training is taking place to correct performance.

E: THREE MONTHS' REVIEW

Prior to meeting with the employee for the three month's review, you may want to meet with the new employee's supervisor, to find out how well he or she is adapting to the job, including attendance, performance, and conduct on the job.

This is important because after you meet with the employee at the three months review period you may decide "this is not someone I want in my department" or "this person can turn out to be a good employee" with a little help, close supervision, and some guidance.

According to OSHA, before assigning staff to work in a hazardous environment or to operate or use machinery, chemical products or electrical equipment, supervisors must ensure:

1... That the employee has undergone specialized training in the use of such machines, chemicals, electrical systems, lasers, tools including how to enter confined spaces, operate forklifts, work in elevated locations, or perform similar jobs, etc.

2... That the employee's workplace is free from hazardous elements and that the employee is safely performing the work.

3... That all workplace mishap is immediately investigated and corrected as necessary and that precautionary action is taken to prevent recurrence of on the job accidents.

NOTE: For more information on safety in the workplace check OSHA requirements and guidelines.

WORKERS COMPENSATION

Accidents slip and fall often happen on the job daily. Some companies may have a worker's compensation or disability benefits while others may not.

Check your company's rules and seek advice from management or HR about this issue.

INJURED ON THE JOB

FOR SUPERVISORS:

If you are injured on the job, seek immediate medical attention, and report the accident to management as soon as possible. However, if you are unable to do so, have a family member report the accident to management and HR.

FOR EMPLOYEES:

If an employee is injured on the job, the supervisor should seek immediate medical attention for the employee and either stay with the employee or assign someone to stay with the employee until help arrives.

The supervisor should then visit the scene of the accident, take corrective action to present future incidents and conduct an initial investigation into the circumstances surrounding the accident. Before leaving for the day, the supervisor should complete the accident report, attached all information to the report and send it to HR or to the head office for their review and action.

C: BENEFITS

To receive benefits, staff may be required to submit to a medical examination by the Workmen Compensation Board's Physician to ascertain whether benefits should be granted.

Employees who are injured on the job will need to:

1. Submit a doctor's note indicating diagnosis and prognosis, and their anticipated date of return to work, and,

2. A written request for the use of sick leave credits or for a leave of absence (with or without pay) until cleared to return to duty by the Workmen's Compensation Board's Physician or by their own physician.

Chapter 12:   RECRUITMENT AND SELECTIONS

A: Hiring new employees can be challenging for new supervisors.

If you work in a governmental or municipal agency check with HR for their procedure for filling vacancies. If not, do the following.

Review all applications, resumes, and cover letters received.

Check and compare applicant's education, experience, and skills with the job description of the position in question.

Plan for the interview, including a list of sample questions to be asked of the applicants.

Complete the Interviewing Form during the interview process to avoid future questions or problems when you do appoint an applicant.

B: CONDUCTING THE INTERVIEW

Listed below are some sample questions to ask the applicants after the introduction which you may find helpful. For example:

What can you tell me about yourself?

What are the three most important attributes or skills that you believe you would bring to our company if we were to hire you?

What is your strongest vs your weakest strength? Where do you see yourself five years from now?

Tell me a time when you had to carry out a task with someone who was particularly difficult to work with.

What motivates you? How would you resolve a problem with no rules or guidelines?

If I were to call your supervisor/co-workers, what would they say about you? Why are you leaving your current employer? (If the applicant is employed.)

Is there anything else you feel I should know about you? Do you have any questions for me?

Finally, thank the applicant for coming to the interview and let them know that they would be hearing from you soon.

NOTE!! Please refrain from asking questions about an applicant's race, color, sex, gender, religion, creed, national and ethnic origin, etc.

BEFORE YOU SEND OUT THE "JOB OFFER LETTER"

DO THE FOLLOWING AFTER THE INTERVIEW

1. Check the applicant's credentials again.

2. Check and confirm the accuracy of the applicant 's References.

3. Do a background check, if appropriate.

4. Compare the applicant's skills with that of the job description.

In addition, do yourself a favor, call the applicant's references, especially his or her prior supervisor(s) and have a confidential chat with him or her regarding your prospective hire. Ask about behavior and how well they work with others, etc.

If you find that the answers to your questions are somewhat evasive, or glorified, watch out.

Believe me, you will either be shocked or relieved that you DID NOT send that job offer out. Make sure you discuss your impressions and the information received from your phone calls with your superiors for their advice and action.

Very important: In addition to the above, you may want to revisit the recommendation letter of your prospective hire. My experience has been that management sometimes will give a glowing recommendation to a "Bad" employee just to get rid of him or her.

Chapter 13:   UN-ANNOUNCED SUPERVISORY ROUNDS

All Supervisors should be making regular and unannounced rounds during their tour of duty. Supervisory rounds should be documented in Communication books, Supervisory notebooks, Shift reports, Ward journals, etc. Documentation for the record should include your signature, date, time, and any problems reported to you during your tour. This type of documentation is especially important for patient care.

In addition to the above, you should have the person in charge of the area accompanied you on your rounds. You should check to make sure that the department or office is operating in compliance with established rules. Have the person going with you to sign, date and time on the report next to your name for the record. This will be your CYA just in case an employee makes a claim that they told you of a problem while you were making your rounds and you did nothing. In addition, you should have a checklist with you to check off the following:

.... Checked Assignment sheets and work orders

.... Total number of employees on duty, awake, alert and performing their duties

.... The environment is free of hazardous obstacles.

.... No problem reported during my rounds, or

.... The following problem(s) was reported and corrected by the supervisor of the department.

.... The following problem(s) need to be addressed by management

.... Original Report of rounds sent to the main office for review by HR with the following attachments,

.... Leave a copy of the documents with the Department.

A: DEALING WITH UNACCEPTABLE BEHAVIOR

Some people learn very early on that the more NOISE they make the more likely those around them will respond to them. These individuals use their bodies and voices to intimidate others. They are your indecisive, resistant to change and are hard to work with employees. How you deal with these employees will depend on your supervisory skills.

B: CORRECTING INAPPROPRIATE BEHAVIOR

To correct unacceptable behavior, supervisors must communicate their expectations to the employee by meeting with the employee to discuss the inappropriate behavior, including:

.... Counseling the problem employee in writing

.... Evaluate and follow up to see if the performance
or the behavior has Improved

.... If the behavior has not improved, the supervisor should
then recommend the employee for disciplinary action up to and
including termination from service.

PERSONAL PROBLEM

If the supervisor suspects that there may have been a personal problem, then the supervisor should give the employee information about EAP (Employee Assistance Program) to get some help. Keep the conversation on the problem and do not let it become personal.

C: DEALING WITH INSUBORDINATION

When an employee is assigned to a task and refuses to carry out the directive, it then becomes the responsibility of the supervisor to immediately:

1. Give the employee a direct order in the presence of a witness (a staff member or another supervisor) if available.

2. Advice the employee that their failure to carry out the order is an act of insubordination and will subject them to administrative action including termination from service.

3. Remind the employee of the rule to "Work now and Grieve Later." If the employee continues to refuse to carry out the order, the supervisor should immediately assign another employee to complete the job.

4. Advise the employee that he or she will be placed on leave without pay for the day.

5. Have security or another supervisor escort the employee to HR and verbally report the incident to management.

6. Before leaving for the day, you should send an incident report with all pertinent documentation i.e. witness statement(s), timesheet and assignment sheet, etc., to HR for their review and action.

7. Keep a copy for your file.

Chapter 15:   COUNSEL – VS - DISCIPLINE

A: Counseling is done at the discretion of the supervisor UNLESS the incident is being investigated and or the act which the employee has committed warrants disciplinary action:

Cause for supervisory counseling:

Poor attendance- Poor Performance- Lower Level Misconduct

WHEN NOT TO COUNSEL

Depending on where you work, immediate disciplinary action may be required for the following infractions.

1. Gross neglect – Patient abuse, Theft of any kind

2. A physical altercation with supervisors or co-workers

3. Deliberate dereliction of duty, job abandonment

4. Gross insubordination

5. Sleeping on the job

6. Deliberate unprofessional or inappropriate conduct which disrupts the smooth operation of the facility.

    Examples: screaming- cursing- threatening- taunting, etc.

If you are not sure when to counsel, consult with management or your HR department. Many of the challenges of disciplining a wayward staff can be eased with a reference back to stated expectations.

B: CONDUCTING A COUNSELING SESSION

FIRST: Before the counseling session with the employee, the supervisor must:

Collect and review all information regarding the violation or the matter to be discussed with the employee.

Give the employee notice of the meeting specifying time and date.

Let the employee know how long the meeting will last.

Send the employee a statement about the purpose of the meeting.

Prepare questions and subject for the meeting that should be covered

Conduct the counseling session in private.

SECOND:

Before the arrival of the employee have a chair ready and ensure the position where the employee faces the supervisor is without obstacles.

Have your secretary hold all calls and keep visitors from interrupting the counseling session. Greet the employee in a friendly, unhurried manner

THIRD:

Be direct. Do not beat around the problem when talking to the employee. Give the employee an opportunity to explain his or her version of the incident or circumstances about which you are concerned.

Keep an open mind. If after talking to the employee, you decided that your concern was misplaced, say so. Explore how the employee can overcome a performance or a shortcoming.

Focus on the employee's behavior, not his or her character, and never characterize the counseling session as a "discipline" or speak in a punitive derogatory manner to the employee.

FOURTH: If you are **not** going to follow up on the counseling session with a written memo, tell the employee before he or she leaves your office. On the other hand, if you are going to **write a memo** to be placed in the employee's personnel folder, you must let the employee know.

C: WHAT'S NOT TO DO DURING THE COUNSELING SESSION

It is inappropriate for any supervisor to do any of the following when conducting a counseling session with an employee.

For example, do not:

Search for or try to review the information during the meeting.

Call the employee at a moment's notice and expect to have a productive meeting.

Abruptly walk out of the meeting without an explanation, leaving the employee wondering why they were called to your office, or give the impression that you are in a hurry to get the meeting over with.

Have the employee sit between piles of papers and files between the two of you. Do not let your attention wander to other people in the office next door.

Talk about your own problems instead of getting the details needed from the employee, etc.

SERVICE OF THE COUNSELING MEMO TO THE EMPLOYEE

When you serve the employee with the counseling memo tell the employee that he or she has the right to rebut it by putting his/her comments at the bottom of the memo.

Inform the employee that their signature only indicates that they have received the counseling memo and it does not necessarily mean that they agree with its contents.

A: Supervisors should know who their employees are by name, title, responsibility, who is on duty -vs- who is not on duty. To do this, supervisors must:

1. Review all sign-in and out timesheets or clock in or out timecards, to ascertain who has called in and who has not, and the reasons why they are not on the job, and,

2. Address latecomers, early departures without authorization and attendance abusers in a timely manner.

B: GUIDELINES FOR PROCESSING CALL-INS

If you are going to need your staff to call in, you and/or your designee responsible for processing Call-Ins must be available to question callers during the call-in period.

You and your designee must elicit from the employee and not from someone else calling in for the employee, the following information.

Name, title, item number, work location, supervisor, and the reason for the call.

Nature of illness/emergency, e.g. self, family or significant other.

Instruct the employee to bring in proper documentation if they are: (a) going to be more than four days out, (b) Is on documentation for lateness or absences or c) frequent call-ins for family illness or personal emergency.

C: PROBLEMS PROCESSING CALL-INS

If the caller is other than the employee, the supervisor must: 1) Request the caller to put the employee on the phone and 2) request and elicit the information as stated above.

D: IF THE EMPLOYEE IS UNAVAILABLE TO SPEAK TO THE SUPERVISOR, THEN THE SUPERVISOR SHOULD:

Enquire from the caller the whereabouts of the employee, the nature of his or her absence and the reason for their unavailability. Inform the caller that the employee upon his return to work must see his or her supervisor upon their return to work.

Remember to take the name of the person making the call-in for the employee for the record.

E: If the caller is unable to give any information concerning the employee's absence from the worksite, and the employee is not available or refused to come to the phone to answer your questions, then the supervisor must:

Inform the caller that the call is not accepted, and that the employee's absence is considered unauthorized and that he or she will be placed on leave without pay and must-see his supervisor upon return to work.

Follow - up

The supervisor must follow up with the employee to ensure that he or she produces proper documentation for his or her absence from the worksite.

Remember, employees at times, may not want to discuss with you their personal or family medical problems. If this is the case, the supervisor must refer the employee to the front office or HR for a review and action if warranted.

F: IDENTIFYING TIME & ATTENDANCE ABUSERS

The use of sick leave as it is earned.

A series of unscheduled absences associated with sick absences including, before or after pass days, before or after scheduled days of, before or after holidays, paydays, habitual lateness or denied for time-off request.

G: EARLY INTERVENTION

A: Early intervention with employees is a key factor in a time and attendance administration. Supervisors should not wait until lateness or absenteeism is excessive before they speak to an employee. Employees T&A Sheets or Timecards must show a record of lateness or absences.

B: Supervisors should notify employees that abuse of sick leave or absent from the worksite may warrant being placed on "Leave without Pay" and request to produce documentation for all future lateness or absence from the work site for at least three months. That notification must be in writing and a copy placed in the employee's personnel folder for the record.

H: REQUIRING MEDICAL DOCUMENTATION FOR SICK ABSENCES
ALL MEDICAL DOCUMENTATION MUST HAVE:

Date and time of doctor's/clinic/hospital visit,

Diagnosis & Prognosis, date(s) of the inability to work and expected date of return to duty.

SPECIFICATIONS FOR DOCTORS NOTE

Doctor's note must be dated and signed by the attending Physician, on his/her letterhead or Prescription pad and signed on the day of the visit.

Employees SHOULD be informed that they are required upon return to work to submit a doctor's note to their supervisor. Supervisors will be responsible for reviewing and verifying all doctor's note for accuracy, which may include calling the writer of the note.

CONSEQUENCES FOR VIOLATION OF TIME & ATTENDANCE RULES

Employees who abused their time or violates management's attendance rules should expect to receive any of the below-listed action to correct their behavior.

> WRITTEN COUNSELING MEMO
> PLACED ON LEAVE WITHOUT PAY
> REQUIREMENT TO PRODUCE DOCUMENTATION FOR FUTURE ABSENCES
> CONTINUATION OF PROBATION (If on probation) OR
> A REQUEST FOR TERMINATION

J: DOCUMENTATION OF TIME SHEETS OR TIMECARDS

Supervisors will be required to document the employee's timesheets or timecards for all lateness or absences as it is occurring.

T/A warnings

If employees received warnings, written counseling, or requirements to produce documents, the timesheets, and the employee's personal folders should reflect such notation for the record. Failure to do so, you will not be able to discipline the employee. Remember the burden of proof is on YOU!!!

K: IMPORTANCE OF DOCUMENTATION & REFUSAL TO ACCEPT DOCUMENTATION

Documenting for the record is of vital importance for all businesses. You know the old saying." If it is not written it never happened" Therefore if you want someone to do something for you, the best efficient way is to write it down. In this case, there will be no misunderstanding as to who was told what or not.

Documentation of incidents, training, warnings, medical reports, patient charts, change of shift report, etc., are all very important for any company, large or small to avoid future problems.

MANAGEMENT IS REQUIRED TO KEEP COPIES OF ALL MEETINGS, TRAINING, ORIENTATION OR COUNSELING SESSIONS CONDUCTED WITH EMPLOYEES. IN ADDITION, EMPLOYEES ARE TO BE GIVEN A COPY OF ANY CORRESPONDENCE WHICH WILL BE PLACED IN THEIR PERSONNEL FOLDER FOR THE RECORD.

L: REFUSAL TO SIGN

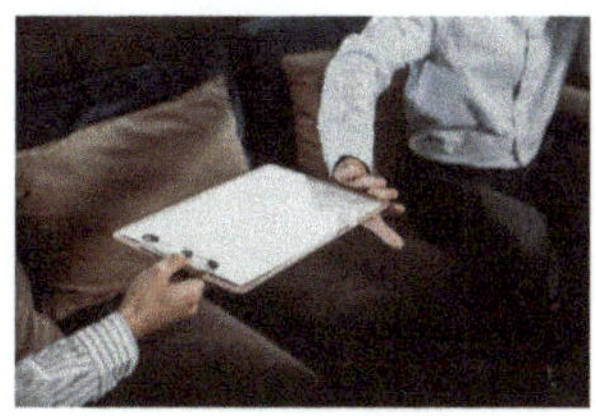

If an employee refuses to sign for receipt of any document when requested to do so by his or her supervisor, it is OK, just do the following procedure:

1. If available, call a staff member or another supervisor to witness the employee's refusal to sign the document.

2. Make a note on the document itself AND both you and the witness sign and date the document.

3. Place a copy in the employee's personnel folder for the record and mail the ORIGINAL to the employee's latest address on file by, "Registered Mail, Return Receipt Requested." and, send a copy of the document by regular mail, just to CYA.

M: RETURN MAIL FROM THE EMPLOYEE

If the mail is returned to the office or to HR, DO NOT OPEN the envelope, just place it in the employee's personnel folder for the record.

N: UNOPENED ENVELOPE

1. The unopened envelope will come in handy in termination or grievance proceedings. This will be management's evidence to show that the employee was offered a copy which he refused to accept and was also sent the original document to his latest address on file and by regular mail.

2. In addition, the unopened envelope will show that the employee did not pick up his or her mail and or refused to sign for receipt of the same.

Remember all employees are required to update their address and phone numbers on file.

SUPERVISORS are required to conduct performance reviews and planning sessions with all EMPLOYEES including probationary, temporary, or seasonal employees on a regular basis.

Job Description: Employees should be given their written job description of the standards and tasks within three weeks of their appointment. This will alleviate any future misunderstanding or problems as it pertains to supervisory responsibilities and what is expected of the employee.

Supervisors should KEEP a folder for each employee who is on Probation and plan to meet with the employee in a timely fashion to discuss and agree on new goals and objectives, and if appropriate areas for improvement.

<u>Probationary and permanent employees</u>:

Supervisory sessions should be conducted at least three times a year. Three months, six months and at the twelve months final period. Supervisors may conduct informal performance reviews and planning sessions more often if they choose.

For the probationary employee, the six months period is very important. This is where the supervisor will let employees know how well they are doing or not.

A: WHEN CONDUCTING REVIEWS, SUPERVISORS SHOULD:

Conduct the session in private, including:

.... Review of task, goals, and achievements.

.... Give the employee constructive criticism about work-related issues or lack thereof.

.... Discuss ways the employee can accomplish new goals or learn new skills, or recommend additional training, if appropriate.

.... Notify the employee of the next evaluation date.

B: EVALUATION RATING

.... Give the employee a rating, "Effective or Needs Improvement."

.... Both you and the employee sign and date the report.

.... Give the employee a copy and file the original in the employee's personnel folder.

C: If there is a need to counsel the employee for task, standards or behavior, the supervisor should do so during the evaluation session and document the same for the record.

D. UNSATISFACTORY PERFORMANCE RATING DURING PROBATION

However, at the 12 month's evaluation session, if you find that the employee is not working out despite being given many opportunities to change behavior or conduct, then the supervisor should seize the opportunity to get rid of that employee during the probationary period before it is TOO late.

It is unfair for supervisors to wait until the 12-month's evaluation period to give an employee an "unsatisfactory" rating. If you do, you will have a grievance on your hands which you WILL not win.

Polls have shown that the actions of supervisors are the No 1 – cause for workplace anger. These same polls have shown that employees get angry because of:

Mistreatment
Unfairness
Disappointment
Nuisances

B: THE PERPETRATORS –-WHO ARE THEY?

You've seen it on TV and read it in the news, many of these perpetrators who commit these violent acts in the workplace are DISGRUNTLED employees who were either laid-off, fired or terminated from their jobs. Some may have experienced unfairness OR injustice because of their employee's status.

Unfortunately, many of these disgruntled employees have in many cases returned to their former place of employment after being terminated and commit murder. According to statistics, 25% commit suicide after the violent act.

FIRST:

SUPERVISORS SHOULD BE AWARE OF THE 'RED' FLAG

If an employee displays a dramatic behavior or personality change and suddenly becomes hostile, it is VITAL for the supervisor to find out why the change has occurred.

Employees who are chronically disgruntled, blame others for their problems and perceive unfairness or injustice may become violent. If an employee makes intimidating comments, threats, or allusions to violence against others in the company, there must be an investigation and appropriate action taken up to and including a referral to the Employee Assistance Program to correct the behavior.

SECOND:

<u>KNOW THE BASIC RULE FOR VIOLENCE PREVENTION</u>

The basic rule for violence prevention is to:

1. Treat everyone with respect
2. Vary your daily routine
3. Report every incident to management
4. Trust your gut feelings
5. Try to spot trouble before it starts
6. Always follow proper security procedures, and
7. At the first sign of trouble, call for support and help

PREVENTION WORKS:

Management can help in this process by checking the confidential background of new employees BEFORE they are hired. Management can also implement a zero toleration attitude to threats, intimidation and any acts of violence in the workplace.

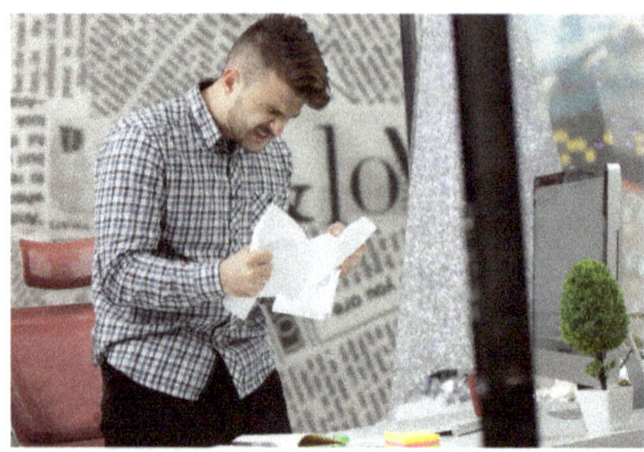

DEALING WITH AN IRATE INDIVIDUAL

Third: When faced with an irate or uncooperative individual you should:

.... alert safety and another staff/supervisor
.... stay alert
.... try to calm the individual down by talking to them.
.... NEVER TOUCH THEM
.... keep a safe distance from the person
.... watch for a verbal or physical sign
.... leave yourself an escape path
.... talk slowly and softly
.... listen to the person
.... offer the person choices
.... do not try to be a hero
.... Call for support at the first sign of trouble

IF THIS DOES NOT WORK

.... Step back and seek supervisory intervention on the scene. Refrain from engaging in a verbal or physical confrontation with the irate individual.

Chapter 19:   WORKPLACE CONFLICTS

A: Unfortunately, conflicts in the workplace has become commonplace. Everywhere you go you can see conflicts between coworkers and supervisors, supervisors and management, customers and employees, arguing, yelling, screaming, and sometimes getting physical with each other.

As a supervisor, you are responsible for enforcing management's rules, regulations, policies, and procedures. In addition, you are the person about whom or to whom employees complain.

How you handle employee complaints will affect productivity and morale. Supervisors need to focus on the problem and separate the personalities from the issues. They should try not to take complaints as a personal affront.

Here is my take on reducing conflicts in the workplace:

- Deal respectfully with each employee as an individual.
- Maintain open lines of communication with employees
  Explain the reason(s) for a decision or an action.
- Recognize employee's performance and give credit when due.
- Be alert and seek out sources of employee's dissatisfaction.
- Take prompt action to eliminate such dissatisfaction, if you can, or discuss it with management.
- Be familiar with the negotiated union/management's agreements, rules, regulations, policies, and procedures.
- Apply the rules fairly across the board.
- Do not play favoritism.
- Re-establish important policy or rule that has not been enforced
- Create an environment that encourages informal resolution for complaints before they become a grievance.

RESOLVING COMPLAINTS AND GRIEVANCES

C: Supervisors are responsible for preventing complaints and grievances in the workplace.

To investigate and resolve complains, supervisors must first do the following:

1.   Pinpoint the problem

2.   Meet quickly and privately with an employee who indicates a problem

3.   Allow enough time, avoid interruption and have calls
     held, take accurate notes throughout the session

4.   Listen carefully, without interrupting
     Show interest, understanding and remain objective

5.   We aware that emotions may run high. Keep
     control of your own emotions

6.   Question skillfully. Ask open-ended questions,
     rather than those requiring a "yes" or "no" answer
     to encourage the employee to present all relevant
     information

7.   Try to understand the employee's point of view

8.   Summarize points raised to ensure a clear
     understanding of the complaint

9.   Ask the employee if you understand correctly

10. Let the employee know when you will respond

11. End on a positive note but avoid unrealistically or false hope

D: PREVENTING SEXUAL HARASSMENT IN THE WORKPLACE

Employers and supervisors are responsible for the sexually harassing behavior of their employee if, the employer or its supervisory staff, "knows or should have known of the conduct UNLESS it can be shown that they have taken immediate and appropriate corrective action to resolve the situation.

It is also illegal for supervisors or management to retaliate against an employee for the sexual harassment complaint. To avoid this type of behavior in the workplace, management must:

1. Screen their employees and conduct a background check before hiring to ascertain if the person they are hiring is the right fit for their organization.

2. In addition, companies must conduct Sexual harassment training for all staff and have a Zero tolerance for conflicts and sexual harassment in the workplace.

3. Complaints received must be investigated immediately and appropriate action is taken, if necessary, even if it is a rumor.

4. Employees who gossip or spread rumors about co-workers and supervisors or engage in sexual conversations that are overheard by others must be dealt with as it is occurring.

Administrative action in such instances would be warranted.

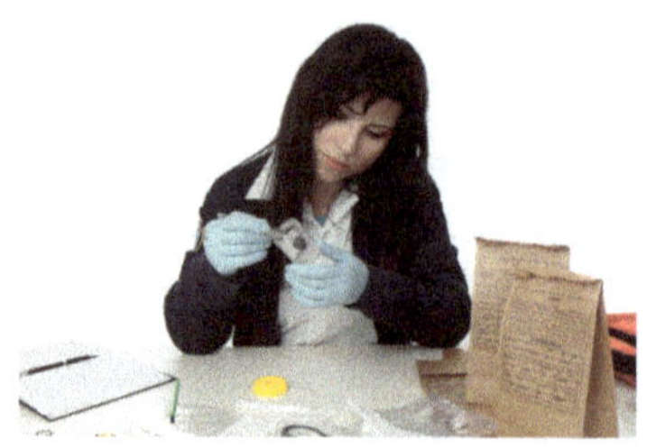

A: One of the many duties of a supervisor is to investigate incidents on the job. This includes investigating, securing evidence, interviewing staff, photographing the evidence, completing a report of findings, and sending it to management for review and action.

Before investigating incidents on the job, the supervisor should:

Develop an investigative plan that consists of an understanding of the facts needed to reach a conclusion, for example:

Develop a strategy for obtaining evidence. This should include a list of potential witnesses and a plan for when each witness is to be interviewed. The order in which witnesses are interviewed is important.

Develop an effective, efficient method to interview principal witnesses last. This will enable you to ask all relevant questions and minimizes the need to re-interview these critical witnesses.

As the investigation proceeds, it may be necessary to review and modify the investigative plan.

To start the investigation, the investigator will:

First: Meet with the supervisor or the person who has knowledge of the incident and will review the Incident Report.

Second: Secure the scene and request all staff to remain on duty until released by their supervisor.

Third: Collect all evidence presented at the scene for the record.

Fourth: Take pictures of the area of the incident. If there are injuries, make sure the person received medical care, and document the information on the Incident report for the record.

B: GET THE FACTS: FOR EXAMPLE:

The nature of the problem- specifics of the allegations (what)

Persons involved –get names and titles (who)

Location of incident-where did it occur (where)

Time of incident (when)

Was anyone hurt, if so, do they need mediate attention?

Where is the injured person(s?)

Who is the person that reported the incident?

Any eyewitnesses(s) (who) staff or visitors/customers

Names and titles of eyewitness (who)

Who was on duty at the time of the incident?

Duties of each of the staff at the time of the incident

Who is the TARGET -vs- VICTIM and location of each?

What information is available to support the allegation currently?

Were the police involved, who called the police and when?

Was management notified, if so, who was called?

Name of a person called, and who made the call?

C: CONDUCT THE INTERVIEW

Prior to taking any statements from anyone, the Investigator will:

.... separate the staff and request that all staff stay on duty until released

.... interview staff individually and in private

.... arrange for another supervisor to take the "target" employee to the office or to HR

.... listen to the staff, ask questions, and take notes

.... give statements forms to all staff present on duty

.... collect statements from the staff prior to staff leaving for the day

.... review statements for accuracy based on your notes taken at the time of the interview.

.... ask more questions (what, where, how, when and who) before releasing staff

.... make sure employees' sign and date their statements

.... tag all evidence collected

.... keep original statements of staff in a secure locked place. Use copies to continue the investigation.

*If Staff refuses to cooperate or impede the investigation consult with your Human Resource Management Office at the time of the refusal. Also, seek advice from HR on how to deal with the "Target" Individual if necessary.

PHOTOGRAPH THE SCENE & THE EVIDENCE

D: Investigators must use plastic gloves for the collection of all evidence. Evidence should be photographed exactly where it is found. (Three photos must be taken as follows);

a. 1....close-up
    2.. medium range
    3.. far (showing location in room/area)

Triangulate location of evidence, document distance, e.g. feet, inches. If the evidence is damp (blood, urine, H2O) allow drying before bagging Use paper or plastic depending on the nature of the evidence.

The photograph must bear the name of the person/object being photographed, including the date, place, time, and signature of the person taking the photo.

COLLECT THE EVIDENCE:

E: THE INVESTIGATOR WILL ALSO COLLECT:

1. Assignment sheets of the employee(s) involved, the incident report, copies of communication books, sign-in and out sheets, logs, journals, etc.

2. Any statement(s) taken from staff and eyewitnesses including any physical evidence found at the scene.

3. Document in the journal or communications book that you have taken the original investigative documents and that you have left copies with HR for their review.

4. DOCUMENT THE CHAIN OF CUSTODY OF THE EVIDENCE

.... Evidence must be properly bagged and appropriately tagged.

.... Evidence must bear the name of the items.

.... Evidence must have the date/time/and signature of the person doing the bagging.

.... Evidence must be hand-delivered to the appropriate individual responsible for the safekeeping of such evidence/property.

.... The person doing the receiving must sign for receipt of the evidence including date and time.

F: CHAIN OF CUSTODY EVIDENCE MUST NOT BE BROKEN

The Investigator handling the evidence must secure a receipt from the person receiving the evidence.

The person receiving the evidence must document the receipt of the evidence and must secure the evidence in a safe place, with limited access.

Anytime evidence is removed, document and secure a receipt from the person taking it including date and time of the person taking the evidence

G: AFTER THE INVESTIGATION

Check relevant contract language and review department policies, rules, and regulations.

Do not confuse impressions with facts when analyzing responses. If unsure, seek management/HR help to resolve the issue(s).

Close the investigation by writing your report and present the facts to management.

Remember to stick to the fact and do not make any recommendation(s). That is for management to decide.

Chapter 20:   REQUESTING TERMINATION

A: All requests for termination must include the following documents.

1. **For Probationary Employees**:

Employee's evaluation reports indicating it was completed in a timely fashion and written comments must indicate "needs improvement" or "failure to meet standards." any written counseling (s) for conduct or performance and a written supervisory request for terminating the employee.

2. **For T/A Abusers**:

Documented proof of written counseling given during the period of the infraction.

Timesheet(s) of the employee indicating absences and lateness

Assignment sheet(s) indicating dates of the infraction (s).

- .. Counseling memos and warnings

- .. An investigative report from the supervisor

3. **Employees conduct on the Job**:

The incident report, eyewitnesses' statements, employee official statement, assignment sheet, T/A sheets, copies of the performance evaluation report, counseling memos and a report from the supervisor regarding the incident.

Any other documentation as it relates to the termination request.

NOTE: All requests for termination must be sent to the HR department and or to your superior. A prior meeting with your superior is commended.

B: Questions to Ask Before You Terminate

According to HR Professionals.com, "before firing anyone, your management should ask the following seven YES or NO questions. If you answer "Yes" to any, your risk of sparking a lawsuit rises, so consider contacting your employment law attorney before proceeding with a termination."

FOR EXAMPLE :

Is the employee over age 40? ☐ ☐

Is the employee disabled in any way? ☐

Has the employee been injured on the job or?

Filed a workers' comp claim? ☐ ☐

Is the employee a minority or a woman with a discrimination claim? ☐ ☐

Is the employee able to claim any discrimination based on? religion, national, origin, ethnicity, sexual preference or other grounds? ☐ ☐

Has the employee filed a discrimination or a?

Harassment lawsuit?

Has the worker been a whistle-blower? ☐

Now that I have given you all the tools, procedures, tips, suggestions, insights, and techniques to help you on your road to success, I trust you will use them wisely AND always remember the following.

There are many reasons why management may want to terminate your services. Some may be your attendance, your performance, your supervisory style, or your conduct on the job. If this is the case, you may want to pay attention to the below warning signs which you may notice before the arrival of the "pink" slip

A: KNOW THE WARNING SIGNS BEFORE YOU GET FIRED:

FOR EXAMPLE:

- A change in management's interactions with you

- Your presence at daily briefings are no longer required

- Instructions are being given to you via email

- Your assistant is being asked to represent your department at confidential meetings

- You are asked to train junior staff to be your backup.

- Your colleagues are acting "strange" around you, etc.

B: CONCERNS FOR YOUR JOB:

If you have any concerns or your job situation is making you uncomfortable, start updating your resume, look for another job and consider QUITTING before you get fired. Your chances of getting another job would be greater if you were: Laid-off – because of company downsizing, closing, or Resign for Personal Reasons, e.g. to take care of a sick family member, going back to school or moving to another job or State.

REMEMBER: Your work history becomes part of your resume and you may have to explain yourself at future job interviews and at the unemployment office, the reason(s) as to why you were fired.

BAD NEWS, YOU'RE FIRED, NOW WHAT?

Just in case you were to get yourself fired as you try to climb up the supervisory ladder, do not dwell on it, pick yourself up, dust yourself off and move forward. I know getting fired or laid off from your job can be devastating.

On the other hand, it may be just what you needed to make you realize that you are no longer an employee or a friend to your staff, but a part of management. If you wish to make a fresh start here are some thoughts for you to consider.

FIRST: YOU CAN START BY REFLECTING ON YOUR MISTAKES OR LACK THEREOF.

Start by reviewing your actions and mistakes which caused you to get fired in the first place, e.g. **Your behavior–attitude–conduct–or lack of skills.**

Revisit your goals and develop a plan to restart your career. **Consider** getting another profession or use your experience as a learning tool, and, **try not** to make the same mistake again. **Consider networking** with friends, colleagues, and family members to help you get that second chance.

SECOND: FOR FUTURE JOBS BE CAREFUL WHAT YOU SAY:

Remember never to talk bad about your past or present supervisors, or the company during the interview, even if you are tempted to do so.

If you cannot say something nice or good, say nothing at all. If you do, you may have a problem getting the job. In addition, never post your anger about your job, your staff, co-workers, your superiors, or management on your social media. Remember it can be used against you in future job prospects.

Good Luck on getting that second chance as you go forward in your journey to the top.

Appendix # 1   BRAIN TEASERS FOR NEW SUPERVISORS
WHAT WOULD YOU DO?

The names used in these situations are fictitious, but the situations are real.

Situation 1: Challenging your Authority

Your director instructed you to give an assignment to Ms. Smith, one of your assistants. You went to her office and said to her. "I would like you to please complete the performance report for these 12 employees." As you were about to hand her the files, she looked at you and said, "I don't take instructions from you, go tell Mr. Jones to " come to tell me himself"? You reported her message back to your director and his response to you were, "you're the supervisor, just make sure she gets it done."

Question: How would you deal with this individual to get the assignment done?

Situation #2 - Testing to see how much they can get away with

You are having a meeting in your office with a staff member who is complaining about Sam, another employee. You called Ms. Roberts, the Senior Clerk in charge of employee's personnel folders and asked her to please send over Sam's personnel folder to your office right away. You waited for almost 15 minutes, no file. You walked over to the records department and said to Ms. Roberts, "Where is the file I asked you to send over?" she pointed to the file cabinets and said, "The files are in the cabinets, you can get it yourself."

Later in the day, you discussed the incident with your director. His response to you was "Who is the supervisor? "Just write her up."

Question: How would you handle this situation? What action would you take if any, on Ms. Roberts?

Situation # 3 First day on the job.

Your first day on the job was met with your assistant walking into your office with a box full of files. She laid the box down on your desk and said, "These are some of the cases which need to be reviewed". Before you could say a word, she closed the door behind her and left.

Question: What would you say to Mary or do regarding this situation?

Incident #4: Failure to cooperate in an investigation

In investigating an incident which occurred in Department A, you approached John, who worked in Department A and was the last person to be interviewed. You introduced yourself and began by explaining why you needed to talk to him. Before you could finish your explanation, he said to you; " I don't know nothing," "I wasn't there." "I didn't see anything" and I am not signing anything either" and began to walk away.

Question: How would you handle this situation?" What would you do or say to this belligerent employee?

Situation 5: Supervisory Sexual Harassment

Suddenly, one morning you came to work and was told your boss has been reassigned and a new Administrator is now in charge of your department. Several of your co-workers were laid off, demoted or terminated.

You were fortunate in that you did not get demoted nor laid off, instead, you were promoted and given a departmental title and a new office. As you were in the process of settling into your new position, the new administrator came to your office, stood behind you and started to rub your shoulders with both hands. All a sudden, before you could say a word his hands were in your blouse.

Fortunately for you, you were able to stop his harassing behavior by saying to him "what the hell are you doing?" He looked you straight in your face and said: "I thought you knew why you were promoted ".

Question: What would you do or say to this person? Remember he has your job in his hands,

Situation 6: Challenging your authority

While reviewing some documents completed by your assistant, you realized that you needed to get some clarification from him. You dialed his direct line, but no one picked up. After calling again with no answer, you called his secretary and said to her, "Please tell Bill to come to my office now." A few minutes later, the secretary called you back and said: "Mr. Thompson said to tell you, he's busy."

Question: What action will you take to correct this behavior, if any and why?

Situation 7: Too many bosses

You noticed lately that you have been getting instructions from several of your superiors including from the CEO to complete various assignments. A few of these instructions are being given to you personally and by via email. Before you could wrap your head around which project you should do first your immediate supervisor came to your desk and said, "start working on the project I gave you, I need it no later than tomorrow." You finally realized that disobeying your boss's orders while at the same time ignoring the CEO directives would land you in trouble.

Question: What would you do, if anything, to resolve this situation?

Appendix 2:   INTERVIEW FORM

During the interview process you may want to complete this form to CYA, and for future reference -just in case.

Position:__________________   Candidate'sName:____________________

Interviewer's Name: _________   Interview Date: _________ Time _________
The candidate has the necessary education and/or training needed for the position

Exceeds requirements--_________   Meets all requirements _________

The candidate does not have the training or education needed for the position

_________ No prior experience related to the position

_________ Do not meet requirement for the position

======= RECOMMENDATION:

_________ Meet requirements for hire for this position

_________ Does not meet requirements for hire for this position

_________ Will keep the application on file for Future Openings

After the counseling session, supervisors must document their meeting with the employee for the record and for future reference. Listed below is a SAMPLE of a Time and Attendance Counseling Memo:

COUNSELING M E M O

TO: ---

FROM: ---

SUBJECT: T&A Abuse

DATE: -----------------------------------

This memo is to confirm our meeting on…………..when we met to discuss your abuse of the facility's Time and Attendance Policy as it pertains to your lateness and absences from the worksite.

Specifically, we discussed the fact that during the period from………to……… you have been absent from your worksite on ……. occasions and were late ……. times even though you were spoken to on at least two occasions, i.e. on-----------------and again on------------.

During our discussions, we agreed that effective immediately, you will make every effort to report to work on time and not be late.

I explained to you that should you continue to abuse the attendance rules, I will have no choice but to place you on leave without pay and need you to produce documentation for every absence from the worksite, for a period of 3 (three) months. I trust this will not be necessary.

Received: Employee Signature ___________________ Title: ________________
        Date ___________ Supervisory Signature_____________________
        Employee's Comments –-

Cc. Employee Personnel Folder/File

STATEMENT FROM EMPLOYEES ON DUTY

AT THE TIME OF INCIDENT

DATE_________ TIME_____________ PLACE____________ SHIFT___________

Employeesinvolved:_______________Witnesses:____________________

Allegation: ____
____
____
____
____

Instructions: Please state (1) where you were; (2) what you were doing (3) what you observed, (4) what you were told and by whom, and (5) what you know of the above incident.

My name is _______________ I am a _________assigned to _____________.
On __________at approx. _________I was ______________________________
____
____
____
____
____

The above is a true account of what I know of the above incident to the best of my recollection and knowledge.

SIGNATURE_________________________________ Date: ___________

Print Name: _____________ Title: _________ Interviewer's Name:___________

IF MORE SPACE IS NEEDED PLEASE CONTINUE ON BACK OF THIS PAGE OR ADD AN EXTRA SHEET. STATEMENTS must be signed, dated and given to the Investigator at the time of the Interview.

FORMAT FOR AN INVESTIGATIVE REPORT

TO: ____

FROM: _______________________________________

SUBJECT: NAME OF TARGET ENPLOYEE/INDIVIDUAL

DATE: _______________________________________

    INTRODUCTION: ALLEGATION

    BODY: STAFF INVOLVED

                      WITNESSES INTERVIEWED

                      DOCUMENTS REVIEWED AND COLLECTED

COURSE OF THE INVESTIGATION :

FINDINGS AND ANALYSIS: BASED ON FACTS NOT FEELINGS

SUMMARY:

CONCLUSION: BASED ON THE EVIDENCE

WRITE THE REPORT :

MAKE NO RECOMMENDATIONS:

SUBMIT YOUR WRITTEN REPORT WITH ALL ATTACHMENTS TO HR OR

MANAGEMENT FOR THEIR REVIEW AND ACTION.

BIBLIOGRAPHY (1975-2011)

TRAINING, WORKSHOP & SEMINARS TAKEN FROM

NYS Department of Civil Service, NYS Department of Education, NYS Governor's Office of Employee Relations, PEF (AFL-CIO), CSEA (ASCME) and COUNCIL 82, NYS Office of Mental Health, NYS Management Confidential, NYS Department of Mental Retardation Including various training and workshops from FL State Mediation and Arbitration Programs.

Courses Taken: ---------------------------

Special investigation- patient abuse & employees conduct

Time & Attendance, Family Leave Administration

Changes in the workplace

Time Management

Effective Communication

Incident reporting

Dealing with Difficult Employees

Counseling & Interviewing Techniques

OSHA: Safety in the workplace,

Documentation of medical records,

Human Rights Complaints and Sexual Harassment,

HR and Labor Relations Procedures

Grievance Administration and Effective Negotiations.

Resolving Management and Unions Conflicts in the Workplace

Albany Law School – Presenting Arbitration & Advocacy Skills

Cornell University – Conflict & Grievance Resolution

Queens College Law School - Introduction to Law

NYS CERTIFIED TRAINER IN THE FOLLOWING AREAS

Special Investigations

Basic Supervisory Practices

Sexual Harassment, Human Rights & EEOC Guidelines

Discipline and Grievance Administration

Conducting Interrogations

Employees Performance Evaluation Administration

Conflict Resolution and Anger Management

Time & Attendance and Family Leave Administration

Presenting Arbitration, and

Mediating Grievances.

■ © 2008 HR Specialist

www.TheHRSpecialist.com

https://friendlystock.com/free-clipart.

Review hundreds of documents from many of my training programs

to put together this Survival Guide for New Supervisors.

OSHA Guidelines for safety in the workplace.

Photos are the sole and exclusive property of Bibi N Bac.

https:/Dreamstime.com Licensed to Author- images purchased for use in this book publishing- Acknowledgement to Kittisak Jirasiggichai; ALbertshakirov; Aurar; Show face; Jason Stitt, Andor Bujdoso; Anan Sudsaithong; Tatiana Kostenko; Msphotographic; Rawpixelimages; Snowingg; Yorgy67; Andrey Papov; Kolapatha Sengbanchong; Mast3r, Antonia Guillen; Fizkes; Marcos Calco Mesa; Wovebreakmedia; Ltd; Edgars Sermulis; Katgezna Bialasiewiez; Fsstock; and, Tsyhun @ Dreamstime.com.